# Why is grass green?

**DK Direct Limited**
**Managing Art Editor** Eljay Crompton
**Senior Editor** Rosemary McCormick
**Writer** Alexandra Parsons
**Illustrators** The Alvin White Studios and Richard Manning
**Designers** Amanda Barlow, Veneta Bullen, Richard Clemson,
Sarah Goodwin, Diane Klein, Sonia Whillock

# Contents

**Why are plants important?**
4-5

**Why do plants grow up, not down?**
6-7

**Why do we need rain forests?**
8-9

**Why is grass green?**
10-11

**Do trees have skin?**
12-13

**Can you tell how old a tree is?**
14-15

**Why are Christmas trees called Christmas trees?**
16-17

**Why are flowers brightly colored?**
18-19

**Why are sunflowers called sunflowers?**
20-21

**Why do apples have seeds inside?**
22-23

**Do mushrooms have seeds?**
24-25

**Why are cactuses prickly?**
26-27

**Mickey's mind teaser**

# Why are plants important?

Because without them we wouldn't be able to live on this planet. Plants take in gases which are harmful to us and give off oxygen which we need to live. And, as if that weren't enough, they provide us with food. They deserve a big thank you.

**"Do re me!"**
Some scientists believe that plants like music. They think that plants grow stronger if music is played to them. But it seems they like classical music better than rock 'n' roll.

**City plants**
Cities need trees and green parks. All the different plants make the air better to breathe and they look nice, too!

### Plant these facts in your brain

 The nettle plant stings to stop animals from eating it.

The giant Amazon water lily has leaves the size of a rowboat. It grows to this size in just one year.

5

# Why do plants grow up, not down?

Plants need light to make food. That's why plants grow from inside the dark earth up toward the light. When they reach light, a plant's leaves open. Then the plant uses the light to make all the good things it needs to grow.

## Growing up

Maybe you've got a green thumb. Collect some seeds or beans. Put some soil in a pot and plant the seeds or beans. If they have enough light, air, and water, they should grow.

## Growing down

There is one part of a plant that doesn't grow up, and that is the roots. They grow down. Their job is to hold the plant in the ground and to pull water, and food, up through the soil.

### Startling seedy facts

 The biggest seed in the world comes from a palm tree called the coco de mer. The seed can be more than 18 inches long and weigh as much as a three-year-old kid.

# Why do we need rain forests?

Rain forests keep our air clean by taking in gases that are harmful to us. They also control the world's weather by releasing moisture into the air which falls as rain. But thousands of acres of rain forests are cut down each year so that people can use the wood and farm the land that is cleared. Many people are worried about what will happen if the rain forests disappear.

## Rain forest people

People have been living in rain forests for thousands of years. They have learned to live with the forests and not to destroy them.

## Fruits of the forest

We also need rain forests because many medicines are made from plants which can't be found anywhere else. There are a lot more plants there waiting to be discovered.

## Remarkable rain forest facts

 Rain forests help to stop flooding by soaking up water and holding it in the ground.

 Rain forests are home to thousands of people, animals, and plants that can't live anywhere else.

# Why is grass green?

Because like every green plant it has a special green chemical in it called chlorophyll. This green chemical – along with a little water and some fresh air – helps plants turn the sun's energy into food. Well, the kind of food plants like, anyway!

### Time to drop off
In the fall, leaves die. They die because they stop making chlorophyll. And that's why the leaves turn orange and brown and wrinkly.

## Great green facts

☞ There are 10,000 different kinds of grass in the world.

☞ We eat a lot of grass – wheat, barley, corn, rye, and oats. They are used in flour, cereal, and other foods.

## Munch, crunch!

Not all plants are happy with just air, sunshine and water. This Venus's fly-trap likes to eat insects, too. When an insect settles on its spiny green leaves, the trap shuts and the insect is stuck behind bars!

# Do trees have skin?

Yes, they do, but it's called bark! Like our skin, bark protects the tree from knocks and bangs and keeps moisture in. As the tree grows, new bark grows with it. The new bark pushes the old bark outward. So the oldest bark is always on the outside of the tree.

### Floating bark
Bark is light, waterproof, and it floats. Native Americans made their canoes out of strips of birch bark.

### Tasty trees
If you tap a hollow tube through the bark of a maple tree, a sweet syrup will drip out called maple syrup. It's delicious on pancakes!

### Tree doctors
People called tree surgeons take care of trees. When a tree is injured, they put black sticky stuff, called pitch, on the part that's hurt. This protects the tree until new bark grows.

## Woody facts

☞ Chomp, chomp! The very first set of false teeth were made out of wood.

☞ Rubber comes from a rubber tree.

☞ Cork comes from the bark of a cork tree.

13

# Can you tell how old a tree is?

You certainly can. Every year a tree grows a new layer of wood. The new wood makes a ring around the old wood. If you count the rings, you know how many candles to put on a tree's birthday cake.

## Counting the rings

You don't have to cut a tree down to tell how old it is. Tree surgeons drill a hole in the tree and pull out a small piece of wood. Then they count the rings.

HA ha ha!
What makes a tree noisy?
Its bark!

## Chief tree

The biggest living thing in the whole world is a sequoia tree in California. It would take 12 grown-ups holding hands to form a circle around it.

## Terrific tree facts

 A large oak tree has about 250,000 leaves on it. Every single one will drop off in the fall.

Tree roots grow thicker and longer every year to support the tree as it grows.

# Why are Christmas trees called Christmas trees?

Because long ago, in Germany, people decorated fir trees as a way to celebrate the Christmas holiday. But long before people celebrated Christmas, they used to decorate their homes in winter with evergreen trees, wreaths, and garlands to remind them of spring.

**Pretty cones**
Pine cones grow on pine trees. They hold the tree's seeds. People sometimes use the cones to decorate their Christmas trees.

**Lucky kiss!**
Mistletoe has been thought of as a "lucky" plant for over 2,000 years. Today we kiss under the mistletoe to bring us good luck.

**Christmas pun**
What do you
call a girl who sings
Christmas songs?
**Carol.**

## Celebration facts

Winter is a busy time for holidays. Jewish people celebrate Hanukkah by lighting candles to remember an important time in Jewish history.

Hindus also light candles to celebrate the Festival of Diwali, which is a time to think about peace.

# Why are flowers brightly colored?

So birds and bees will notice them and sip their nectar. (Nectar is a sweet liquid found inside flowers. Bees make honey out of it.) While creatures are drinking the nectar, pollen from the flower sticks to them. Then they carry the pollen from flower to flower. The pollen then goes inside each flower to make seeds.

**Don't bee funny**
What did the bee say to the flower?
**"Hello, honey!"**

## Stink bomb

The biggest and smelliest flower in the world is the rafflesia. It's as big as a truck tire. It smells like rotting meat. Flies love it – yum, yum!

## Night flowers

Some plants have flowers that open only at night. These flowers are usually a pale color and have a strong smell. This is so creatures that are awake at night – like bats and moths – can find them.

### Flowery facts

☞ The largest rose tree in the world is in Tombstone, Arizona. Its trunk is 40 inches thick, and it is nine feet tall.

☞ The American ragweed plant can make eight billion pollen grains in five hours.

19

# Why are sunflowers called sunflowers?

Because they look like small suns and because they "follow" the sun. During the day, sunflowers turn their heads from where the sun rises – in the east – to where it sets, in the west.

**Hey, speedy!**
Sunflowers grow from small seeds to flowers that are taller than most people – about six feet tall – in less than six months.

## Sunny sunflower facts

 The largest sunflower ever grown was in Holland. It was almost 26 feet tall.

 Sunflower petals are used to make yellow dye.

Just one sunflower head can have more than 1,000 seeds.

## Useful seeds

Farmers grow sunflowers, not because they look pretty, but because their seeds are used to make cooking oil. The seeds are also good to eat.

# Why do apples have seeds inside?

So they can grow more apple trees! The seeds get bigger inside the apple and stay safe until they are fully grown. When the seeds are ready, the apple falls to the ground. Some are eaten by animals and some just rot away. Eventually some seeds find their way into the ground and start to grow a new tree.

## Seed food

Coffee and chocolate come from ground-up seeds, and so does pepper. Achoo!

## Tree seeds

Nuts have seeds inside their shell. Squirrels collect nuts and put them away to eat later. Sometimes squirrels forget about their nutty hiding places, and so the nuts stay in the ground and grow into trees.

### Seeds take a hike

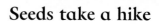 Some seeds – such as dandelions – are carried away by the wind.

Some seeds have little hooks that stick to animals' fur and get a free ride to another place.

# o mushrooms have seeds?

No, they don't. Mushrooms and toadstools have things called spores instead. These tiny spores drop to the ground and grow into copies of their parent mushroom. The wind also carries the tiny spores far and wide, so mushrooms grow wherever they land.

**Mushroom alert!**
Never pick mushrooms. They could be poisonous.

**Important fungi**
Mushrooms and toadstools are part of the fungus family. This fungus, called beefsteak fungus, grows on trees. It looks just like a piece of uncooked steak!

## Mushroom facts

 Some members of the fungus family have great names such as, stinkhorns, earthstars, and puffballs.

 The largest mushroom ever found was in Ohio. It was 77 inches wide and weighed 72 pounds.

**A mushy joke**
What's the smallest room in the world?
**The mushroom!**

# **W**hy are cactuses prickly?

To frighten off any hungry birds or animals who might like to take a nibble at the flowers. The spikes on a cactus are really its leaves. They usually grow in little groups around the flowers on the cactus. The spikes are long and very sharp.

**Watch those spikes!**
Cactuses live in very dry places such as deserts. If cactuses had ordinary leaves like other plants do, they would dry up in the hot sun.

26

**Desert flowers**
In spring it rains and the cactus flowers get ready to bloom. Their flowers blossom between June and December.

## Spiky facts

☞ Native Americans in Arizona used to use cactus spikes as pins.

☞ The biggest cactus in the world is ten times taller than a person.

☞ In Mexico, hollow giant cactuses are used as a place to store grain – prickly spines make them mouse-proof.

27

# Mind teaser

Look at the pictures. Can you remember which plant doesn't have any seeds?

**Answer:** The mushroom.